How I Loved GOD and Her
The Battle of the Heart

Monica Williams

ISBN-13: 978-1-970079-09-8

Cover Designed by Darius Barnes
Live Life Creative | Graphic Communication & Design

Edited by Driadonna Roland

Published by Opportune Independent Publishing Company

Opportune Publishing is a full-service book publishing company that focuses on non-traditional authorship. It is our business to keep a diligent emphasis on quality and precision, while always allowing innovation and creativity to seep through. Unlike many other publishing companies, all genres are welcomed here.

For permission requests, write to the publisher, addressed "Atention: Permissions Coordinator" to the address below.

Email: Info@opportunepublishing.com
Address: 113 N. Live Oak Street
Houston, TX 77003

DEDICATION

To my mother Jeanette Wilkins-Kennedy, father Dock Richardson, stepfather Willie Kennedy, grandmother Anna Wilkins, cousin Melvin Terry Jr., uncles Lawrence Wilkins and Roy Carter, I know you all are rejoicing in Heaven. Love and miss you all so much…

CONTENTS

CONTENTS

ACKNOWLEDGMENTS

I would like to take this time to thank some awesome people who helped make this dream come alive. I want to particularly thank Marcella Richardson for showing an interest in my dreams of writing and publishing a book. A few days after I shared that I wanted to write a book she called saying, "Start on your book. Write three pages. Do more if you are led to do so, but start with at least three pages and keep adding until you are finished."

I took her advice and started writing. She held me accountable by calling and texting every few days to make sure I was still on track, so thank you for the encouragement and the push that was needed to start me on my way.

I would like to thank my coach, Nikkie Pryce, for taking time to invest in the birthing process of my book. You believed in turning my dream into my reality. This has been a journey I was uncertain I would ever take, let alone finish. Thank you for guiding and encouraging me through the process. Like you said, "Dreamers, Take Action."

My spouse, Juanika Ballard, was one of the people telling me years ago to start writing my book, but of course life kept getting busy and I would come up with countless excuses not to write. The drive and motivation just was not there at the time, but she never gave up encouraging me. When I finally started she was more excited than I was. She would stay up listening to me as I read pieces of our story. Thank you for being my inspiration and rock through it all.

Thanks to my family for always believing and supporting me through any and everything. Although they did not initially know I was writing the book, they still played a vital part in helping me. I did not want to share with my Aunt Wilma or cousins Trina and Kia until I knew the book would be published; I wanted to surprise them so they would be proud of yet another accomplishment of mine. However, I ended up sharing the news and their responses were priceless! Love you all to the moon, stars, sun, clouds, and back.

My children are so very special and dear to me, the bond is unbreakable. There are barely words to describe the love I have for my sons Anthony, Demetrick, Kenji, and Sohn, and my daughter Surae. I have to be a continual example to them so they will always believe anything is possible and never give up on their dreams—no matter how long it takes, they do come true.

My youngest sister Danielle Kennedy is my love, she encourages me to never give up. As I was writing I was reminded of her words, "God will not give you more than you can bear." I had to trust and rely on God's strength and not my own to get me through as my sister did and still does so many times in her life. Thank you for showing me how to rely on God when I felt overwhelmed with writing. Unbeknownst to her, her strength in God gave me strength not to quit.

Thanks to my sister Tara Richardson and brother Andre Richardson for their support, encouragement, and love.

Thank you to my handful of amazing friends: I love you all for always supporting me without hesitation. Y'all know exactly who you are and so do I. You all believed in me no matter what and held me up under pressure. I love you all dearly.

Thank you to all of my Millersville University professors for building my confidence as a nontraditional student and motivating me to never give up.

Last but certainly not least, thank you Courtney Bennett. There are no words to describe how grateful I am to you. I shared with you I was writing a book and your exact words were, "Oh mom, I am so excited! Please let me edit the book." You have spent countless days and hours making sure everything was perfect. You took on this project selflessly as your own. You cared, nurtured, and helped bring it to life. Love you.

INTRODUCTION

How I Loved God and Her is my story about being a Christian woman who shares life with another Christian woman. The struggles, pain, and triumphs of it all led to a desire to trust God in a way I never had before. The struggles pushed me into guilt, shame, and condemnation; the pain caused sleepless nights, tears, and uncertainty. Meanwhile the triumphs gave me a sense of who I was, who I was to become, and the acceptance of God's unchanging love.

I'm choosing to be transparent with my story because you never know what telling your story will do for you or someone else. I don't know why God loves me, but He does and that gives me hope. So many people have a story but are afraid to tell it. Sharing this particular story with the world is nothing I ever imagined doing. I always knew I would write a book about my life, but never in a million years did I think this would be the story told. I wanted to share what my life really was and not what I pretended it to be. I would rather be denied for who I am than to be accepted for who I am not. So many of us are being accepted and invited for who people think we are, then denied when who we really are shows up.

The world gets to experience while reading my story the authenticity of my heart and truth. While I was trying to hide the life I was living, I made myself believe the most loving God had somehow stopped loving me in the midst of it all. I realized we all have our own cross to bear. Yours may look different from mine; nonetheless it's still a cross we must carry to the end in order to complete our purpose.

God is not done with me or you yet; the period has been mistaken for the comma. Our stories are "to be continued"...

CHAPTER 1
Love at First Sight
(Was it Real?)

Seated next to my husband in the second to last pew, I noticed Her as she entered service. Captivated, I watched as she drifted down center aisle to an end seat. At first glance my perception was, *She's beautiful*. I found nothing wrong with this train of thought, a mere observation.

She was tall, brown skinned, and almond eyed and had long dreadlocks. A uniqueness about Her struck me. For reasons unknown, I was mesmerized. The police uniform? Her facial expression, straightforward, strong, and bold?

I remembered thinking, *This woman appears gay*. She conveyed both appealing masculinity and comforting femininity; the attractiveness alarmed me. To examine Her in such a way, in church nonetheless! On the surface, she was a "strange woman," someone I should have remained unaffected by. There was no apparent or legitimate reason as to why I was so taken or moved by Her, yet my attempt to control these thoughts proved unsuccessful.

The pastor called those willing and in need to the altar. She stood up and I continued to follow Her every move as she walked to the front of the church. I asked myself, *What might she need? Deliverance?* In that moment, I recognized the parallel in what I assumed to be our shared desires. Pastor prayed for Her, and as she cried, I felt an involuntary sadness as it fell upon me. I saw the pain and struggle in Her eyes as she wiped away Her tears. I felt the urge to reach out and hug this stranger as she retreated back to Her seat.

Despite great efforts to remain focused, I could not

take my eyes off Her. Feeling contempt toward myself, I wondered what exactly it was about Her that compelled me to feel this way. My husband at the time put such questionable ideas in my mind about what a companion should provide, relay, and teach. But during this service, I forgot my husband was sitting next to me. I suddenly realized my thoughts had not included his presence once.

Sooner than I would have liked, the church service was over, yet my feelings followed me home. My husband exhibited so many insecurities, displayed so much unhappiness that it was easy to resort to thoughts of someone other than him. One evening about one or two weeks later, I dreamt about the woman I had seen in church that day; this made me all the more confused. I settled with the fact that week after week attending church I hoped that I would see Her again, yet I did not. This beautiful creature of wonder, appearing larger than life and out of my reach. Where was she? I had more than noticed Her, but had she seen me at all?

A number of Sundays came and went; I desperately hoped to see Her again if only to get just another look at her beautiful face.

I could not comprehend the connection I felt with this woman. *A woman?* I would ask myself. *What is this?* I questioned Him, on more than one occasion. *She's a "she," not a "he," and I am a married woman who loves her husband although he is not always deserving. Me, a Christian woman, who knows better than to be overtaken by lust!*

I started to think of Her increasingly, even when I did not want to. I listened to people speak about the first time they encountered their husband, wife, boyfriend, or girlfriend. Love at first sight? I'm already married. To entertain the thought of love at first sight seemed silly and childlike, removed from who I was and what I represented during that time in my life because I no longer responded or acted on impulses. I had always been a steadfast woman, true to my convictions yet still a dreamer. Love at first sight was an inconceivable concept that I left to fairytales and movies only. Carrying this woman in my heart was odd, unrighteous, and uncomfortable.

I couldn't define what was happening to me at the time—nothing added up. She had infiltrated all of me without my permission; she occupied my attention, my mind, and my heart. Thoughts of what could be with this stranger fostered growing resentment toward my husband, who had for a while proved our marriage was a mistake. Our union was headed down the drain early on as I realized his bachelor tendencies had never fully come to a close. He was a cheat and liar, and I felt deceived and wronged for believing this man would fulfill me.

Despite what I already knew of him, I still had reservations about my thoughts surrounding this woman; thinking of her caused me not to think about the dreadful pain in my heart from my husband. Just as I began to feel emotional refuge in my dreamlike thoughts of Her, my husband of 15 months found our home unbearable to live in any longer. He walked out on me and my three sons, which I had from previous relationships, taking everything he walked in with including my two stepdaughters, 6 and 8. What little happiness I had been able to cling to over the past few months shattered in a million pieces with his abandonment.

The blame I placed on myself was never ending. My self-image was destroyed. I questioned why I had not worked harder to lose weight, eat less, appear sexier in the eyes of my husband so that he had no choice but to erase his thoughts of other women. Where were my self-control and discipline? I convinced myself that my constant nagging and inquisition of his whereabouts forced him to stray, forced him into the arms of someone else. I'd lie awake at night thinking, *You should've shut your mouth and prayed more.* Silence was never one of my traits; until this moment I had always considered this fact a strength. Standing your ground was essential where and how I grew up. Now I observed my gregarious nature as simply crippling, a handicap causing me to be left alone.

I told myself repeatedly, *You should have been more patient with him, eventually he would have done what was right in the marriage when he was ready.* I concluded it was my fault that he ultimately left.

At the same time I was left wondering, *Where is she?* I became infatuated with the idea of Her and how she could uplift me despite the fact that I didn't know Her from a can of paint. It is so ironic how we can place so much value and significance upon people we know nothing about.

Yet I questioned whether she could remove this pain I felt without having knowledge of its origin. I felt worthless and wanted to retreat to a place of solace, far away from my reality. I felt my life had no value. My heart was ripped to pieces along with my self-esteem and confidence; all three so low that I was uncertain whether I could recover from this. Day in and day out, I suffered constant heartache, longing to be accepted, noticed, validated, and most importantly loved. I was lonely, scared, and depressed; I shut myself completely off from the world. I refused to punish anyone by sentencing them to the presence of my misery.

My husband's family and I attended the same church, the very church where I first saw Her. I began to learn that my husband had tainted my name, blaming me for our failed attempt at marriage. Guilt-ridden, I felt defeated by his words, which proved stronger and rang louder in the ears of his family, our church community—and with enough repetition, in my own my mind. I continued to go to church but with my head held down in shame, praying I would go unnoticed. I prayed he wouldn't show up and wished harder that his family would walk past me without an outward display of pity.

Each Sunday when church concluded, the exit seemed miles away and my feet seemed unable to move beyond a snail's pace. I would cry as soon as I reached my car, only to retreat home to my room in order to submerge myself under the covers. I felt most secure under this cloak of solitude. One thought gave me life: *Would I see Her again?*

Why was I still thinking about this woman? I had no idea who she was and it reached the point where I wondered if she had ever really existed. I began to grow concerned at whether or not I was becoming delusional. Throughout our relationship, my husband had done a good job convincing me of this. Even with valid proof and solid corroboration, everything I approached him with was denied with his unwavering confidence and disloyalty. As wrong as it felt, keeping my vows to this man ultimately seemed like the right thing to do, hence my hesitation with these recent thoughts I was experiencing.

I pleaded with God to take him away from my heart, close this chapter, and help me to move forward in my life. Without ceasing, I prayed to God to end this pain, heal my heart, and mend my brokenness, relieving me of the agony of my aching soul. Could someone truly love me as God did? As of yet no one had. I was used to love using and abusing, coming and going, disappointing and letting me down, and being inconsistent. Love as I imagined it was sinking in the ocean, never to be found by me.

Was love out there waiting to find me? How would it look? The only love that ever remained this far was the love of God, and I needed it. But I couldn't help but wonder, could romantic love between two people happen for someone like me?

I was not ready for another relationship anytime soon, but I continued to pray for the allowance that someone would love me just as He did.

CHAPTER 2
Dreams Do Come True
(No Matter How Brief)

Ministry served as a part of my recovery during the divorce process. One afternoon, I was invited to a gathering by one of my fellow church members. I initially accepted the invite with haste, but when the day arrived, I felt extremely tired from the day's events, running around taking care of things my children and I needed done. I had finally arrived at a place in my life where normalcy was returning.

As I was making my way back inside the house after a long afternoon, the constant chime from my cellphone was becoming a distraction, somewhat of an annoyance. A close friend appeared several times on my log, texting, "Where are you? We're waiting." I assured her I was just too tired to be a good guest at a party, yet she persisted and I caved after a few moments, annoyed I had been so easily swayed. I stopped along the way to purchase dessert, reluctant to show up empty-handed even for a short stay.

When the host opened the door, I smiled with restraint, entered the household, transferred my dish to the kitchen counter, and looked out into the living room with an expression short of despair. What I saw next, I am still hardly able to describe in perfect form. Seated at the dining room table, hand to mouth, partaking in a crab feast: Her. "How are you here?" I voiced to myself. She served on no particular ministry that I knew of, so why was she present? Who had invited Her?

Through small talk, I realized the person hosting the gathering was in fact her mother—quite a beautifully awkward moment! The entire evening brought nostalgia of my high school years, complete with remnants of butterflies in my stomach. My mind raced with so many questions: *Is she looking at me? Does she think I'm cute? Am I Her type?* And then…*Why in the world are you worried about whether or not she's looking your way?*

Clinging to my reservations, I reminded myself that I was not attracted to women and immediately began to create a wall of doubt, insisting these ideas were a mere result of the post-traumatic stress associated with my separation. I was married the first time I saw Her; this time I was in a different space, separated and soon to be filing for divorce.

The evening went on as we laughed loudly, ate plentifully, spoke openly among each other. I avoided Her one on one, but I could feel Her occasional stares throughout the night and honestly, I enjoyed it. At the same time, I couldn't help but to feel that my desperation was more transparent than ever. I began to feel self-conscious, worried that I was misdirecting my need for attention. Was I willing to sacrifice my integrity for attention no matter who or where it came from? Was I truly enjoying this moment?

I shut my mind off for a moment and then realized that the majority of the people at the gathering had left. It was only Her, her mom, another young lady, and I who remained to continue our discussions. Although I could not reveal it, I wanted the night to go on forever in Her presence. Was I losing my mind over this woman I had just barely come to know within the last three hours?

At the end of the evening as I watched Her walk toward Her truck and open the door, I wanted to hop in the passenger seat, begin our journey together, drive to OUR home together. I drove home thinking about Her the entire way, unshaken in fantasy.

The next day I called her mother to thank her for the invite and let her know how much I enjoyed the company. As we continued conversing, I said, "I didn't know Her was your daughter; she is hilarious." Then I surprised myself—before we hung up, I gathered the courage to ask for Her number.

I waited a few painstaking hours before calling. No answer. I left a message, taking care to leave my name and remind her who I was. After hanging up, I grinned from ear to ear, hoping she would return my call soon. Later that evening she called but I was in the shower... I rejoiced thinking the missed call would mask my eagerness. In an attempt to contain the butterflies in my stomach and regulate my heartbeat, I listened to the voicemail she'd left me three times before I called Her back and we finally linked.

As happy as I was to reach out, it was just as easy to keep the conversation going. We spoke of all the fun we had at her mother's gathering, how well the food was prepared, how long it had been since we'd laughed that way. As I was listening to Her voice the thoughts in my head were far from holy. We hung up far too soon and agreed we would talk again sooner. The next conversation we had was both about nothing and everything. There was an air of avoidance of things unsaid but longing to be mentioned; we danced around what truly occupied our minds. Nevertheless, I enjoyed the time spent learning one another, however superficial.

Our next encounter was at Sunday service, which was both comforting and invigorating. She walked to the altar for prayer and returned with tear-brimmed eyes. I waited to console Her with the acceptable "church hug" before she sat back at Her seat. What came next was unexpected—a close embrace occurred as she lay Her head on my shoulder crying and allowing me that moment of vulnerability. I was speechless at first but grew comfortable as I consoled Her and reminded Her that things would be OK. She proceeded back to Her pew but somehow it seemed in our spirits and hearts as though we sat side by side for the remainder of the service. I couldn't help but to believe our hearts and emotions matched one another.

The Turning Point

Walking out of the church, we spotted each other. She asked whether I needed a ride to my car and I accepted Her offer. The short ride to the distant parking lot seemed to fly by. "Thank you," I said as I reached to get another feel of Her, to be a little closer to Her. I asked what she would be doing for Father's Day and we both talked about our plans of how we would celebrate with our dads.

Later that evening, I made the phone call to Her that would serve as a "game changer." I dialed the numbers hoping she would answer; I waited to hear "hello" and my heart dropped. Immediately, from the time we greeted each other, our conversation took off and led to an all-nighter. No topic went untouched: dreams of what future careers might bring us, our upbringings, our favorite foods.

Eventually, we hit the climax we had been building up to for the past couple of hours—sex. It changed the dynamic of our conversation as I posed, "I need to ask you something... Are you..." She responded without a need for completion, "Yes, I'm gay." Startled, I wondered how she'd known I would be forward in asking so early on about Her orientation. "I already knew what you would ask me," she said. Embarrassed for unknown reasons, I blurted, "Well just so you know, I don't look at you any differently."

My thoughts raced, *Now what?* By force of habit, I spit out, "If you need someone to talk to or pray for you, I'm here." Instantly, I regretted the statement. How could I pass such judgment and insinuate she needed prayer for being attracted to women? Wasn't I attracted to Her despite my lifelong convictions? I didn't know how to come clean about what I was feeling without projecting guilt onto Her; it was an awkward predicament.

I was not ready or prepared for the conversation we would have next. She revealed that she didn't think I would be the person of choice to pray for Her—she feared that to pray with me on this matter would be a conflict of interest. I felt a pinch of disappointment and a tinge of excitement combined. "Of course I would serve as good council," I said. "I'm a good listener, a wonderful prayer partner…" I counted out these characteristics I thought I exhibited. "You wouldn't be able to pray with me about my sexuality because of the way in which I'm attracted to you," she replied.

"And what type of attraction would that be?" I asked, becoming as giddy as a junior high student recently courted by the most popular guy in school, the first of many lusts and infatuations, the most significant. I yearned to hear more of how she thought of me, wishing I could reciprocate. But she expressed that it was not a good idea to converse with me for the purpose of healing Her insecurities. In my mind I was thinking, *Tell me more, feed my insecurities, pick me up out the gutter, build my self-esteem—yes, I'm here for all of that!* It meant nothing short of the world to me at that very moment that someone noticed me.

I was still enduring the proceedings of my divorce and the breakdown of my self-esteem. My husband spared no opportunity to describe how unattractive I was, contributing to my plummeting confidence, worsening my depression, and deepening my self-hate. My only refuge was the thought that I was again someone who could be adored, someone who could serve as an object of affection and desire.

Yes, I wanted Her to confess more: What exactly was attractive about me? I required that validation, that assurance that I was not just dying by the wayside. She admitted that my beauty, charm, and smile displayed a certain animation, openness, and innocence when she observed me at her mother's that night. On the other end of the phone, I grinned uncontrollably. She imagined that I had been married and that my husband had spoiled me with lavish gifts and swept me off my feet every chance he could get. I laughed at how far off she was, yet a part of me was happy that she couldn't see just how broken I had become. There was a part of me I needed to keep sacred and private; I did not want to appear completely open for interpretation.

Though Her assumptions couldn't have been further from the truth, I knew that she was the total opposite of my husband and not just obviously because of Her gender. I built my husband up for what seemed like forever only for him to eventually tear me down to nothing.

Portion by portion, I fed Her bits of me, commenting on the ways in which I felt life had not been on my side at this time; I believe she felt genuine sadness for me in those moments. She began an endless tour of pick-me-ups, demanding that I knew just how special I was. I began to convince myself that I mattered to someone, I could be important. My empty soul began to fill back up with kindness, consideration, wellness, and love.

Our conversation lasted hours, and in that time, I smiled and laughed more than I had in months. I felt my body coming back to life and I would not allow myself to lose this feeling. We talked all night but I never tired, only growing bigger and brighter like flowers being watered back to life. Falling asleep would have snatched these moments away and I did not want to wake up only to realize it was all a dream. When the morning arrived, the sun shone and the birds chirped louder than they ever had; we napped only then. It was as if I did not want to conquer the physical or figurative darkness without Her any longer.

In Too Deep

Upon waking up after talking until 5 in the morning, we agreed to see each other later that evening. I was obligated to present myself for traffic court on this particular day but I promised I would visit Her soon after. The anticipation I felt was overwhelming; excitement was an understatement. I barely recall the events of the case or even the judge's ruling as I thanked him and rushed out the courtroom, over to Her.

I pulled up to Her house, removed what felt like spaghetti for legs from my car, and started to make my way toward the front door. The pounding sound my heart made served as competition for a nearby fire truck as I knocked. She opened the door with an inviting smile; I walked in, unsure of what exactly would take place. She had on hoop shorts, a white tank top, tube socks—a true depiction of the star basketball player she told me she had been at Her alma mater. Her dreadlocks were queenly the way they flowed down Her back. Staring at Her caramel skin, I couldn't help but feel like a child in a candy store; I worried whether I appeared on the outside the way I felt on the inside. When she hugged me, I melted, and a whirl of insane emotions overcame me. I never wanted what was happening to end.

After a while, it grew time for me to exit and handle real life at home but I longed for Her to command me to stay. As if she were telepathic, she asked, "Do you have to leave?" I smiled, responding, "Yes, but I can come back later," and I did. Later crawled by but eventually arrived. Back in her home, we were completely smitten with each other. We couldn't ignore the strong feelings of infatuation that suffocated the room.

Without hesitation we acted on those feelings and the dynamic of the relationship changed for what I couldn't decide was for the worse or the better. I was in disbelief about what had happened, but there was no turning back at this point. How would I keep this up without others finding out? How could I make myself believe that it was OK to carry on with this woman? What had I done? What if my children found out, my family? How would I serve as a role model, the eldest of my siblings, a pillar in my church community, and tell myself that this was OK? Yes, I knew that she was a person, but she was not quite the right person—she was a woman. I had fallen in love with a female. But I did whatever it took to mask what was going on with us because I did not want to let this happiness go away.

Imagine love finding you and sweeping you off your feet every single day. I was floating on air and living my life happier then I had ever been. She took me on dates where we enjoyed fine dining at restaurants that I didn't even know existed; I remember going to Ruth's Chris Steak House for the first time.

When we pulled up she opened the door, extended her hand to help me from the car, and safely walked me into the restaurant, then went to park. While I waited for Her to return I said to myself, This is different—people don't treat you like this unless they want something in return. It's not real. When she walked back in the restaurant and gave her name, I saw that she had taken the time to make reservations. She grabbed my hand as we followed the hostess to our table and she pulled out my chair. Again I thought, This can't be real.

The part that really overwhelmed me was the prices on the menu. "Wait, who pays this kind of money for one steak," I said to Her. "Do they serve burgers"? She politely said, "Please don't pay any attention to the prices and order whatever you like." The problem with that was, I was unfamiliar with the cuts of steaks! She helped me order one of the most expensive items on the menu: a Porterhouse steak. By the end of the evening, she gave me lessons on what to do and not to do on a date.

I had been in a few relationships, but they all came with the indirect understanding of "If I give you this what are you going to do for me?" I was not use to something being done for nothing. Don't get me wrong; every guy I dated was not all bad. They just treated me like a lady until they became familiar with me, but not Her. I couldn't believe how much she loved me. We talked daily and she showed a genuine interest in hearing what I had to say.

She was so caring and thoughtful about ways in which she could make me happy. She would cook for me, pack my lunch for work when I stayed over, and make me breakfast in the mornings. On days when our schedule didn't permit overnight visits she would drive nearly an hour one way just to share my 30-minute lunch break with me. I repeatedly asked myself, What type of person is this?!She went out of Her way for me without asking for anything in return. I constantly thought of ways I could repay Her, but nothing compared, all she wanted was my time.

As if loving me was not enough, she quickly developed a bond with each of my sons, especially the youngest one. Being a single parent of an adolescent and two teenage sons was challenging. At times I had to choose between work or being present at extracurricular activities; most times work won. Without hesitation or having to ask she would stand in the gap for me and attend football or basketball games. I wondered what they thought about the nature of our relationship. I introduced Her as a good friend and that is how they accepted Her. She seemed to instantly love them and they appeared to enjoy having her around.

I enjoyed our time together as well. She made it all worthwhile with her endless amounts of surprises. She asked me one day, "What's one of your biggest dreams?" I replied, "To take my kids to Disney World one day," quickly followed by the negative response that, "It will never happen though—that's for rich people. I could never afford that." She got quiet for a moment and I could tell Her wheels were spinning, but we continued on conversing about other things.

About a month or so later, she invited me over to Her home. She said, "Tell me your biggest dreams again," and so I did. "How would you and the boys like to go to an all-expense paid trip to Disney during spring break?" she asked. I became teary eyed; I was in disbelief. She had purchased tickets for every single park, Downtown Disney, hopper passes, and our resort—all I had to say was yes.

She made life for us so surreal and we lived in the moment of happiness and fulfillment. There was nothing I spoke of that she didn't make happen; all my dreams, wishes, and hopes were manifesting right before my eyes. She was everything I had ever imagined, but the woven secret of our relationship was beginning to unravel. As time progressed my boys would ask, "She's your friend, right Mommy?" Their inquiries about the nature of our relationship became increasingly more frequent, and I began to panic. Then the church we attended started spreading what they believed was transpiring between us, and it was getting back to us. I went from feeling on top of the world to being overloaded with anxiety. I did everything I could to convince my sons and fellow church members that what they believed or heard was not true.

CHAPTER 3
It Got Messy
(Who Would've Thought?)

Time after time, we'd both agree, "We cannot do this anymore, we have to stop," but feeling this sense of contentment seemed far from wrong. How do you walk away from something that completes you, picks you up, and erases any self-doubt? I didn't know how to say no to Her and us. She gave me life, meaning, purpose, and an endless amount of smiles throughout my days.

Oh, how I wanted to go back to our happy place together when it felt like she and I were the only ones on earth... walking on air again without a care in the world. Where did we go wrong? We tried to be as cautious as possible. How did we allow our affair to be questioned? When did we start looking like more than friends? Did we spend too much time together? I questioned myself repeatedly. I needed to escape from it all. But who could I talk to and would they understand the kind of love that had found me?

Unable to conceal it any longer, I shared with my sister, cousin, and a best friend what had transpired with Her. Initially, they weren't in total agreement with the relationship, but they were witness to the dark cloud that had been removed from over me; they all concurred that seeing me smile again made them feel good. It felt like a breath of fresh air, to be able to talk about what was going on with someone other than Her, because at times I did not know what to do or how to feel.

With the highs, there were occasional lows: Church Sundays were difficult and filled with denial. Thinking back on it, the measures we took to "right ourselves with the Lord" seem preposterous. At one point, we decided we would no longer see each other on Saturdays so that we could appear in right standing before the Lord on Sunday mornings. This idea was carried out for a very brief period of time. The more time we spent together, the deeper the emotions ran and we found more reasons to see each other every day, however brief.

A day gone by without Her was far too long. I was at Her house, she came to mine, and spending so much of our time together created what seemed like physical sickness in our bodies when we were forced to be apart.

What were we doing? Could this go anywhere? How much longer before the charade was up? I began to fear an inevitable demise where we were concerned. Day to day I went back and forth, up and down, certain and not certain at all. I was completely in love with Her and didn't know how to feel any other way. I didn't want to turn whatever "this" was off. It wasn't fair to throw away the happiness that I felt I deserved in return for all the heartache I had suffered previously. The confusion ate at me consistently. We attended a church that spoke against us, the word spoke against us, society spoke against us, and we too began speaking against us.

We hid what we were to each other from others and she wanted people to know. I grew deathly afraid that we would be found out by other people besides the few who knew. To those unaware of the dynamics of our relationship, we were close friends, confidantes, and prayer partners who had met in church. A few people were not so easily deceived, and when I began to hear what they were saying about me, I would get so upset defending my construed lies.

I could not tell my children because of how they would perceive me. I felt the sharp pains of hypocrisy as I reminisced over all the lectures I had given them that demeaned homosexuality. We'd had conversations over the years where my sons would approach me with stories or questions about companions they had whom they believed to be gay. We would discuss the ramifications of people who chose to engage in same-sex relationships; how could I turn back from that now? There was no other option but to stay secret.

I was completely exhausted and began to question how much I truly wanted this. I never identified as a gay woman, and I wasn't sure how to identify myself. I'd joke, "Why couldn't you just be a man? Why do you love me so much?"

Why was I unable to embrace this? Labeling her a person instead of a woman justified and validated our relationship at times, but it wasn't sustaining enough for me. I had many sleepless nights but they were no longer because of our stimulating conversations, they were now because the stress of it all weighed heavily on my spirit. I would cry and shame myself for allowing this to spin out of control.

We came to a crossroad. Do we move away from everything that was familiar or stay in our uncomfortable comfort zones? I started to physically slip away and my emotions were at an all time high trying to figure out what to do next. Speculation about the nature of our relationship was all around us. From church members, to my children, and acquaintances who knew us, they were starting to talk and it seemed to be spreading like wildfire.

How could I turn this around and fix this when love looked like what I had, but my religious beliefs said something different?

CHAPTER 4
Losing Each Other
(Falling Apart)

Two years in we decided to relocate. The belief that we were living our truth remained with me; after all God is love. But with that faith, I knew others may not share the same perspective. Unfamiliarity somehow had grown to become a comfort zone.

I convinced myself that moving together would be merely a transitional phase. I'd save enough to move the kids into a place of my own and we'd go from there. Come together just to eventually grow apart. The logic was off but it was more appeasing than, "I don't want to be the target for your stones," so I stuck with that. My children would view it this way because that is how I would present it. Roommates. Better opportunity. Simplicity.

Driving out to our home for the first time was surreal. The close of 695 traffic as we neared I-83 and its introduction to an endless stream of open air froze in my mind as I was daydreaming about the soon-to-come transition. I stared out and greener pastures stared back. Welcome to Pennsylvania! Would we be welcomed? Honestly, I couldn't care less about scrutiny from strangers; it was those who knew me whose daggers felt the sharpest. As we navigated through the neighborhood, we passed a farm. I couldn't see where it ended and I wondered how far away from the world one could escape. We pulled into the driveway and an odd sense of stillness ran through me. The house layout placed Her and me in separate bedrooms. Roommates sleep in separate spaces. That is what we do. At the time my children were 14, 16, and 18; ages of exploration and the discovery of the world's truths. The irony of this suffocated me each evening as we said our goodnights and retreated to our designated spots. It became the most difficult task I had to endure. I reasoned that we should remain as friends in the eyes of my children because an open relationship might be traumatic. Retrospectively, this was traumatizing Her and me.

The pressure of hiding us was too great, too hurtful. More frequently my conversations with Her ended in all the same ways: shouting or silence, crying or contempt as a result of my need to remain a secret to my children. It was more than I could handle.

She said, "I no longer want to be a secret," and I didn't know how to honor that request and give her want she wanted. I was not comfortable being open about something I felt ashamed of. Here I am, a Christian woman, knowing more than enough of God's word to know that my lifestyle choices were not pleasing in His sight. I was no longer sure of what I had signed up for and I wanted to get out of this relationship. We had made a hasty mistake in our excitement and acted without thinking things through, moving to another state together as if that was going to be the solution to our problem.

I began to place a great deal of blame on Her. She thought this would make us stronger and cause our relationship to blossom even more. My tone toward her was beginning to take on an air of despise, as if I were some innocent bystander swept away by Her renegade love. I was circumventing my guilt for the love and adoration I had always had and still did have for Her.

I made it a point to mention that I was saving money on the side and looking around for apartment rentals just to make it clear I wasn't planning to stay. At one point, it no longer mattered to Her, or at least it didn't show in Her expression. I loved Her so much, but I did not want to continue hurting Her; I could not give Her what she deserved. Her expectation was love without restrictions and unconditional acceptance, and I could not give her that.

When we were in our separate homes, sneaking around was romantic and exciting. Sneaking around in our home was bondage. She became depressed and showed it outwardly. After a while I had even suggested she go and find the woman who could satisfy Her heart's desire; I wasn't willing to be that. She cried and pleaded for my love and affection as I rejected Her over and over again.

It was just too much for me at the time. The person I fell in love with and could not get enough of had become my biggest headache. The vast transformation from then to now was too much to bear. She had always loved me in a way I'd never been loved before; she uprooted her life for me, revolved her world around me, took care of me, and remained loyal throughout it all. Hell, she was amazing.

I could no longer see her as "a person," but as the woman she was. Identifying Her as a person was universal and ideal, but identifying Her as a woman was reality—a reality I wasn't sure I wanted to live in.

Each day I made excuses for why my actions were justified. Why is she being persistent about this? Why is she making this difficult for me? Why can't she just be OK with the way things are? She should know my stance on this: Go be with someone who can make you happy.

She would grow emotional and accuse me of being detached. "Why do you make me feel bad for loving you?" she'd ask. My responses were pious and superficial: "You should be ashamed, wanting to be with a woman. God does not want this for us. We both need to be with men."

My core ached with shame, feeling horrible for the way I was treating Her. I pushed her further away from me and deeper into depression. I no longer desired Her anymore. When she would want to be intimate, I would pull back. She stopped asking to be close. The honeymoon phase had come to a halt and the dream was officially over.

Two years in our home and I felt every bit of it. The days crept by, and with the time I imagined ways to either reinvent or find myself since everything around me proved I had lost sight of things. I decided to go back to school and enrolled in college the spring of 2008. I became more disconnected emotionally and wasn't around at home as much; school provided me that allowance, which I looked at as a plus. However, with my class schedule I worked less and couldn't afford to save the money I mapped out in my initial plans; this meant a continued shared space, which didn't thrill me.

Something became different a few months into my second semester. I noticed Her efforts had diminished when engaging with me. What once was a common annoyance when we would exchange heated interactions then became an infrequent occasion. She no longer seemed bothered or upset over our arguments; actually, instead of exchanging words she would leave the home altogether. I shook it off and took it for what it was worth; maybe she finally got what I was saying as far as our need to separate.

But what was it I wanted Her to realize? That I had never truly had any feelings for Her all along aside from those which derived from lust or wonder? That Her whereabouts were none of my concern? That we weren't really a family? I knew certainly that wasn't true before, but when had it become true now? I wasn't sure in that moment of anything at all and it terrified me. I didn't like the way I was being forced to second-guess myself and evaluate my thoughts of late. I needed a clearer picture of what I wanted, and just as I thought I was getting it, things became much more foggy than ever before.

I knew I had to decide on whether to love Her or let Her go. What did I really want though? Loving Her was easy, but trying to love God while loving Her was the twist. I wasn't sure how to do it without the convictions. I asked myself, What's really preventing you from being happy? What are you afraid of? Why won't you allow Love to Love you? It wasn't God I was really hiding from—He already knew. I struggled to decide what was best for me because I was more afraid of what it would look like to other people.

Tired of the ups and downs of my mood swings, she started checking out of the relationship. Did I want to risk losing Her forever?

CHAPTER 5
Losing Self
(Am I really Losing it?)

The self-doubt I experienced each day only grew and was later accompanied by suspicion and jealousy. I began to daydream of Her in Her absence where before I pushed Her to the back of my racing thoughts. Something here was quite different.

She was no longer checking for me, asking if I was hungry or calling to see if I'd be home late. I guess she wasn't checking after a while because she was going out so often herself. This wasn't work she was attending to though. No, work never called so late or made Her bust out laughing in mid-conversation while she looked at Her phone. I was being given a dose of what I had dished out and the taste of it was awful.

I was no longer the object of Her affection and it soon became clear that it wasn't shallow in nature. This wasn't a tactic but a genuine distraction. Was someone else in the picture? I had finally driven Her into the arms of another person after all of this time, all of Her tolerance and pain. We had switched lanes and I wasn't prepared for this course. I found myself wanting to pull over and reconfigure the direction we were headed in. I needed to find out what was happening. I started snooping and trying to find the answers to our disconnect. I had once believed she loved me so much in spite of my resistance that the possibility of Her leaving was slim to none; that time was gone. I had believed that despite my resistance toward Her she was not going anywhere.

Intuition of course led me to what my heart was not ready to accept. Time and time again I pleaded with this woman, my best friend and confidante, to leave and search for a new path and a new person to walk it with. Now she was and I grew angry about it.

While I was in my fall semester of school, I discovered that she was seeing someone else. I had never fully gained the confidence I needed to do well as a nontraditional student and now I was struggling with this as a major distraction. My home and class assignments began to suffer and my grades weren't as steady. I struggled to keep up with all the kids fresh out of high school, and I felt like I was always in a competition. Now I was competing for a heart that I never thought I would have to fight for. Now I had to deal with Her not wanting me anymore.

Why was I so angry about the fact she was seeing someone else? Isn't that what I asked for? My heart broke into a thousand pieces. I realized I had lost Her and she wasn't coming back. Losing Her made me realize I had lost my self. I knew how much I loved Her and my mind wouldn't let me think of anything else. With challenging work and my failing confidence, school was proving to be more than I bargained for. Home had never been so cold. I felt myself crawling back into that dark and sunken place. I struggled with my depression, now feeling the pain I caused her.

I needed for Her to love me, and more importantly I wanted Her to love me again, but someone else had stolen Her heart. In attempt to regain Her love, I knew I'd have to do whatever it took and I knew that meant no longer keeping us a secret—but I didn't care. In response to my confessions, she relayed that she could no longer lend me Her heart. She lacked trust in me and believed my territorial nature wouldn't allow for me to see Her with anyone else. I stopped eating; the only thing I was consuming were thoughts of Her with someone other than me. My focus at school diminished to an all-time low. Darkness had taken over my soul and I could no longer see the light of happiness. I missed the way she used to look at me and tell me how much she loved me. I had cared so much about the opinions of others that I had completely neglected the way she was feeling and how she would feel in the future. I had forced love out the door forever.

Months passed and the tip of the iceberg finally melted—a breakthrough. After what seemed like endless silence and confusion, she caved to the idea of giving us another chance. The first thing I vowed to do was tell my children and family about us, placing us back on the right track. With that major reveal, I couldn't help but to wonder whether I was setting myself up for embarrassment. I continued to wonder about the other woman, who was now out of the picture, and I considered how long people had been known to save something to the side for a rainy day knowing they'd seen so many storms in the past. This is an action used by many as a self-defense mechanism. Protection of the heart. Would I ever be able to truly gain full access again?

My insecurities peaked. I was uncertain about our future and continued to feel disconnected from Her. I knew she still didn't trust me to love Her, which I understood.

But as it always does, intuition found its way creeping up my spine.

I soon learned my suspicions had been correct. I found out that she was still seeing the same woman from before, which left me hurt and disappointed, to say the least. My trust issues overruled my thinking in every possible scenario. I questioned everything that was intangible; Her word was worthless these days.

Though she confessed countless times about how apologetic she was, nothing made much of a difference. In search of any opportunity to win my affections, she asked me to marry her and I said yes without hesitation. I felt I had no other options; I was too afraid to say no and risk another fatal setback, risk another chance at losing Her.

Right before my eyes, she planned the whole ceremony. I felt like it had only been three days before I found myself positioned across from the ordained minister, facing both my mate and the waterfront on the coast of New England. It was in fact three months, but the pace of it raised the hair on my neck. The ceremony was breathtaking, precisely detailed, and of course situated on the water—both of us were born under the element. Not a rosebud was out of place in its arrangement, but I couldn't help feeling otherwise. My mind was plagued with doubt as I questioned all the reasons I had said yes in the first place. I had been able to gain back everything I wanted; what else did I need?

Standing at yet another crossroad, I had arrived at a place that I was all too unsure of. Time and the steadfast behavior she displayed in arranging our ceremony let me know the other woman was out of the picture for good, but things didn't get any easier as the days went by. I became angry with myself for being so emotionally unstable that I married someone because I was too afraid of losing them to someone else.

She was devoted and committed to me, making every day a platform for my happiness. She surprised me with endless gifts and tokens of Her appreciation. She was my enthusiast, completely in love and enthralled with me. I, however, grew increasingly anxious. It was torturous going through the motions, learning to trust Her completely once again. I wondered whether Her affair was over for good. Did she truly love me? Was I enough? My mind had become a receptacle for nothing but unwanted garbage; I didn't want to think anymore.

One year into our marriage she said, "I want us to have a baby." I was caught off guard, feeling vulnerable, and anxious to give Her whatever she wanted. It's all we spoke about each day: who would carry it, what changes would exist, what the financial impact would be, among other things. I didn't want to rob Her of the experience of motherhood that I had been blessed with. She really wanted to have a baby and I agreed.

After we decided she would be the carrier, we spent about a year consulting fertility clinics and specialists, preparing her body for the process, and conditioning our thinking for an ideal outcome. We picked a donor and proceeded with insemination as suggested. She began fertility drugs and we waited for two weeks until we learned that we were officially pregnant. We were thrilled—even myself with my anxieties—imagining the life that we would create and nurture. It was exciting and it brought us closer again.

One afternoon we traveled to the lab to have routine blood work drawn. A few days later we were informed of abnormal results and told to come in for further testing and evaluation. "The numbers" were dropping, indicative that a miscarriage might be occurring; our souls were crushed. I watched Her shut down with disappointment. The staff confirmed our worst fears and we suffered through it deeply. I remained the rock as she cried all day and night. We knew that we wouldn't give up and that we'd try again soon.

With two vials of donor sperm left, we were told she would receive a more aggressive form of therapy. We went for insemination on a Sunday, and the minutes and hours and days dragged on for two weeks. Here we were again, in one of our most precious moments of truth, and we were taking another pregnancy test and receiving another initial positive test result. As excited as we were, we shared a common skepticism in facing the reality of our past; joy was interchangeably felt with sadness and contempt. They drew more blood; we awaited more results. The cycle continued, the anticipation worsening with each step taken. "Your numbers look really good, but let's run just a couple more stats…you know, to build our confidence," we were told. It was as if all the staff could feel the anxiety that resonated in our voices when we spoke; they treated us kindly and showed empathy. And then we discovered brand new findings: Our numbers were doubling! No stagnancy, no gray area, no ambiguity, but instead tangible proof of our productivity, our love, our prayers. Our hearts nearly burst out of our chests! We viewed the first sonogram at six weeks.

Do you remember the first time you were actually surprised? Like maybe that first crush in the seventh grade who returned the same adoration that you felt for them? A true surprise is priceless; it evokes the greatest emotions and inspires the most joyous moments. When the obstetrician told us we were pregnant with twins, we were speechless to say the least. At once my maternal instincts drove me into obsession about the way our babies would look and all of their characteristics, quirks, and personality traits. I dreamed of a girl and secretly knew she existed among this newly declared pair.

Our blissful moments were quickly followed by a threat to Her health. She constantly vomited, struggling to keep down mere morsels of anything I prepared for Her. Our assumption was that morning sickness had reared its ugly head. However, the illness continued constantly without warning or parameters. Eventually she was diagnosed with *hyperemesis gravidarum*, a condition causing extreme cases of nausea and inability to absorb vitamins and nutrients necessary for both the mother and fetus' development.

Consumed with the stress of Her diagnosis, we

became all too familiar with technical difficulties, event interruptions, and repeated cancellations with friends and family throughout the pregnancy. When she wasn't confined to the hospital, she was home attached to tubes and fluids. I remained empathetic, but I had never experienced anything like this with any of my boys. I took into account my tender young age of 15 when I had my first child without any complications as oppose to her being in her thirties and made a realistic comparison between what was my circumstances back then and where we were now.

The event that had seemed so far away was firmly here right where we stood. We were 36 weeks pregnant and she went into labor and our twins were born. Smitten, optimistic, and in love, we were excited by our newborn fever.

Reality Was Ever So Present

It was time to bring our twins home from the hospital and we were excited to begin this journey of raising our children together. I could not believe I had two tiny people whom I now had to protect, care for, and love. I was now responsible for making sure I didn't disappoint these innocent babies, and I wasn't sure if I was capable of fulfilling the task. There was a 20-year gap between my youngest biological son and the twins, and when the reality of that truth smacked me in the face it was like I had come out of a trance. There was around-the-clock feedings, diaper changing, and bottle sterilizing, and as luck would have it they were not on the same sleep schedule.

I loved these babies and I never allowed myself to believe otherwise. But I was in my forties, and I was tired; I had raised children all of my life and then some.

Frustrated and angry, resentment crept up on me. I was now a full-time undergraduate student and stay-at-home mom. Meanwhile, she was living the dream working in a full-time position that she had been waiting for since the start of Her police career. I was always at home with the babies, with the exception of time spent in school. It was my daily itinerary, unchanging. I became upset easily, throwing fits and on a few occasions yelling and displaying emotional breakdowns, wanting to walk away from it all. The pressure of starting over as a new mom was taking its toll on me and I wanted out. I was gasping for air all the time, suffocating, afraid that she wouldn't see my point of view. I didn't want to appear ungrateful or disloyal in any way, but I was miserable and could no longer mask it. I was losing control. My peace was obsolete.

She annoyed the hell out of me. I was raising OUR children and she stopped in every now and then after working long hours. She meant no harm, but it did not change how I was feeling. I never wanted to feel like a single mom again, yet I was faced with mommy duty as my daily routine. The demands of Her job seemed to be more important and Her absence was becoming too familiar. God what have I done and why do I feel so alone?

CHAPTER 6
God Doesn't Love Me
(The Abandonment Felt Real)

Growing up I do not recall hearing messages preached against homosexuality, nor was it a topic of discussion in my home. It was not until my late twenties when the church sermons started to resonate with me for the purpose of using them to correct other people with scripture living in the lifestyle. I adopted the ideals against homosexuality as my own when those condemning messages of how God felt about lesbian, gay, bisexual, and transgender people were taught.

When I pursued a lesbian relationship I became a part of a community I too believed God did not love, and that was painful to accept. How I addressed other people with the word of God who were in an alternative lifestyle now applied to me. It was gut-wrenching hearing from the pulpit about how I believed God felt about me. I felt like I was in a bottomless pit unable to escape the intolerance that was being taught. I knew the sin of homosexuality was not a pleasant sight to God, but no sin is. However, this was the only one that seemed to separate me from God, the sin I couldn't recover from, the sin God could not forgive. I never questioned if God loved me until I became who He could not love. Therefore, the distance between God and I grew 100 miles more by the day; at least that's the way I felt. I was calling on Him frequently, asking for help to, strengthen, and lead me to a place where I could feel close to Him. I felt like God was punishing me. I felt alone and unheard, believing that He had turned His back on me as a result of my defiant ways. I was an emotional wreck and no longer felt God cared or loved me anymore. I was plagued with confusion and defeat.

Negativity became a close companion of mine. I wallowed in my despair, believing I knew best the way

God felt about me. I was a sinner who no longer spoke the same language, an unsightly stranger. My recent lifestyle choices had provoked Him to no longer accept me as His daughter. He could not love me while I was loving Her. I felt everything she gave me was good, but God saw it as bad, therefore, the constant struggle between the two remained present.

At the bedside, knees reddened and weak, I opened my mouth to speak but felt undeserving of being able to utter anything to the Lord. I was sure God no longer heard me as I allowed myself to fall into a same sex relationship that He certaintly did not approve of. How dare I ask Him for anything after preoccupying myself with this fling, experiment, or whatever it was at the time?

I believed I was a disgrace. Any time I had to myself was spent crying and digging myself deeper into my woes. I yearned for Him to be happy and accept me as she so easily did. However, you can't have your cake and eat it too. They could not both wrap their arms around me when I felt desolate. I felt I could not belong to both God and Her although I desired this so deeply. When I was without the company of others, I felt truly alone. I couldn't hear Him speak to me anymore as He had my entire life. My back was against the wall feeling I had no option to break free from the bondage of my thoughts. There's nothing like believing you are disappointing God. The idea that He did not love me anymore because I chose Her was so upsetting to me. I needed my heart to be settled and my fears to be calmed. I needed for Him to look at me and be pleased, to smile when I spoke aloud to Him. I envisioned a fixed frown on His face as if I were not a part of Him anymore.

I began to ask questions seeking clarification

about God's will for me. I questioned whether or not God preferred for me to be alone. I mean, my last marriage was snatched from beneath my feet faster than I had time to stop it. Now I was back to square one, alone and afraid under the surface. Although this time, I had created this sense of loneliness. Superficially I appeared happy, satisfied, and content with life, but internally the storm had peaked and my mental environment was in disarray. The relationship I once had with Him I believed had come to an end. It felt dead, but I longed for it to be alive again. Admittedly, although I wanted to restore my relationship with the Lord, I was not willing to dissolve what I had with Her. I was so far from Him and yet I yearned to be closer.

I wanted to be happy with my life, Her, and our babies, but I felt His disapproval in my soul each day. She was feeling the backlash and experiencing the disappointment I felt about myself. I was taking Her on an emotional roller coaster ride, choosing when and where I wanted Her.

Not only was I in a relationship with this woman, our union was solidified with children. She remained an open book about how much she loved me; courageously she offered me the option to live the life that I truly wanted without Her as a smear. She believed she was the cause of me feeling separated from God and she felt disheartened. Feeling as though she had disrupted my life, she didn't want to remain a poison responsible for my predicament. I no longer trusted my decisions or myself for that matter. Nothing gave me enough satisfaction to endure this constant conflict. Just as much as I wanted to let Her go, I feared losing out on all the love I felt radiating from our family. She gave me life, protection, and love. She added happiness and joy; why should I have to give it up?

I often looked at my family and felt, *I cannot give them my all.* How could I love them if God would not love me because of them? It was all too complicated for me. I was believing all I had ever heard about being an abomination, the way it had always been taught to me in church.

Though I persisted in my thoughts, she remained completely on the other end of the spectrum. She wanted us to be on the same page, believing that God had never forgotten about us and that in fact we were living His will by sharing our love for one another. When those refreshing moments were present I enjoyed my life, children, and Her. I wanted to embrace Her wholeheartedly, treasure Her heart which was positioned right in front of me. She loved me with Her words, Her actions, and Her soul, but she was also doubtful about whether or not she should continue to care for me unconditionally.

She had loved me with everything she had to give and I wanted to do the same.

She was good to me and loved me in a way I have never been loved before. Her love was fairytale love, knight-in-shining-armor love, out-of-this world love. God also loved me beyond my wildest dreams, showing me time and again that His was the kind of love I could not live without. Why was this a battle? Why was I in turmoil? Why did I have to choose His love over the love of my life? The cup of happiness I had always prided myself in holding was becoming more diluted every day, growing weaker. It grew difficult to contain my internal struggle, and I became visibly frustrated. It became an emotional strain that caused mental and physical exhaustion for the both of us.

We never wanted to separate, but staying together seemed so difficult, especially when everything around me was screaming louder than the love in my heart for Her. I spoke my feelings to Her in silence and cried for Her when we were apart. Loving who you love should have been easy; instead it became increasingly painful because I didn't know how to shut off the voices in my head telling me how awful I was for loving Her.

"Being deeply loved by someone gives you strength while loving someone deeply gives you courage."

—Lao Tzu

Yet, during our estrangement, there continued to be an unspoken understanding that we weren't supposed to ever give up on each other.

CHAPTER 7
Turning off the Noise
(Peace Be Still)

Everything around me was too loud, undesirable, irritating to my soul; this version of me was unbecoming and I had to shed myself of it. I told myself the baggage must go along with the doubt and fears; disbelief had to be turned off.

How do I begin to quiet what was around me? That which controlled my existence, mind, and heart had overpowered me for far too long. The noise was always louder than the silence, and over time I had become in sync with its sound and beat. I had become used to the blues. Responding to the noise was more comfortable than being at peace with the stillness of God's voice.

I think about the avenues which God takes to reach us, and it is marvelous. I remember running into work late one morning, frazzled and exhausted after a whopping four hours of rest the night before. It was raining, weather I appreciated usually, but today another source of anxiety. The previous Saturday I had spent what seemed like an entire shift at the hair salon just to walk out flat-ironed; to ruin it in one trip from car to door seemed ridiculous. I sighed, struggling to expand my umbrella in order to avoid getting wet.

I approached my desk and spotted a note that read, "Let me know when you are available to talk." *My supervisor?* She was far from a micromanager, respectful of my work ethic and more pleasant because of it. I tried to think back to all the events that had occurred Friday afternoon before I left the office. With school and its demands, I found things were constantly lapsing in my memory and I grew concerned that I had forgotten to complete a task. Immediately, I went to my supervisor's office and knocked lightly on her door. Before I knew it I was sitting in front of her teary-eyed, yet not for any reason I had ever imagined.

My supervisor invited me to sit down with her. We stared at each for a couple of moments. I felt awkward, almost as if I had the word GAY written on my forehead. Was this woman coming on to me? I laughed at the thought right after; it was good to be able to smile at something this morning even if only to myself.

"I'm not sure how you're going to take this, and I don't know if you're a believer or not, but the Lord woke me up at 3:33 in the morning," she said. "The Lord specifically instructed me, *'Tell Monica I love her.'"*

Sitting there with a puzzled look frozen on my face, I couldn't tell what angle she was coming at me with. She continued, "That is all He said, nothing more and nothing less."

In that second everything quieted around me. I could hear a pin drop just before I began to weep uncontrollably. Oh my God! I confessed to her that I knew the reason He would say such a thing, although I withheld anything else. She knew nothing about my struggle or me for that matter and it wasn't her job to, however, she had been utilized for a purpose—His purpose—because that was the way He had intended it.

My tears fell to the floor along with any doubt about who He was. At the close of our discussion she offered,

"He will never leave you nor forsake you, Hebrews 13:5." She assured me no matter what I was going through *God had never left my side.* The words rang truer than anything I'd ever heard: *God loved me.* In an instant I felt His love again, listened to the sweet sound of it in my ears. God's love for me had never diminished, but my faith had once it was clear He wouldn't accept me due to my choices. Even though I always knew He was a loving, kind, patient, and gentle God, He needed me to be reminded because I had still allowed others to bear weight on my judgment.

It was I who turned my back on God when it was difficult to face the music. White noise drowned Him out and prevented me from receiving any clarity. His love for me meant everything, comparable to the love from one's parent. It was easy to come to this epiphany because of the love I have for all my children. There is absolutely nothing that has ever prevented me from loving them, whether they were right or wrong. Loving a person does not equate to agreeing with all their decisions or enabling their wrongdoings but just the opposite, in fact. Creating consequences for their actions, teaching them to be virtuous, and instilling love and forgiveness in their hearts is what I did to convey my love for my children. This is all God ever wants from us; it's all He ever wanted for me.

My two eldest children took me to hell and back when they were young, still finding themselves and growing further and further away from me. It is difficult to imagine that you could ever be distant from a person you gave birth to but yet and still it happened, yet it was not because I didn't love them. Whatever consequences they had to bear, my love was always there just as I was. To this day, to hear them thank me for having their back is both heartwarming and humorous as if a punch line were dropped. *Of course I love you, you're my son,* a parent thinks to herself. In that moment, I was able to draw the parallel.

At times the world around me seemed bigger than He did. I wrestled so much with the woman I loved and the God I wanted to serve. There was no way I could do both, I believed. I always heard you could not serve two masters; you either love one or hate the other (enemy). Being in a same-sex relationship caused me to disconnect from God because I felt as though it did not align with His word. I was astonished, even then, at His grace and mercy—giving me what I didn't deserve and not giving me what I did deserve, His love instead of His wrath.

Turning off the noise allowed me to see myself outside of my situation instead of in it. In order for me to see God in me I had to see myself as more than my circumstances. God will not always immediately change your situation, but He will change you in your situation, which can ultimately change the world around you. I wasted precious time consumed with believing God did not love me because of the lifestyle I was living. I was reminded of the promise that He never left me nor did He forsake me; no matter what I thought He was always by my side.

Turning off the noise allowed my spirit to awaken again. It put me in touch with feeling His presence and opened my heart to receive the blessing I had been blocking: God's Love. I no longer wanted to be running scared but standing boldly in the face of the man I knew loved me; His name was Jesus and I longed to be in His will.

Romans 8:38-39 (New Living Translation)

And I am convinced that nothing can ever separate us from God's love. Neither death nor life, neither angels nor demons, neither our fears for today nor our worries about tomorrow not even the powers of hell can separate us from God's love. No power in the sky above or in the earth below indeed, nothing in all creation will ever be able to separate us from the love of God that is revealed in Christ Jesus our Lord.

I absolutely hated that I allowed myself to believe God had stopped loving me. He sent His only son to die for me while I was yet a sinner. God's love was different from the love the world showed me, but I found myself at a crossroad not being able to distinguish between conditional and unconditional love. Therefore, all love carried the same weight and God somehow became equal to human love. I'm so glad I came to the realization of what it's like being loved by God and knowing it could never be compared.

CHAPTER 8
Back Together Again
(He Was There the Entire Time; Psalm 139)

I saw my father for the first time when I was 9 years old, again when I was an adolescent, and then periodically throughout my early adulthood. My father passed away in 2006 when I was 34 years old.

Despite his absence, I loved him unconditionally; this could very well be the reason it was so easy as a child to accept God's love though I had never physically seen him. It was not a surprise that I later struggled with abandonment and questioned whether or not God would leave me the way my father had. I desired to be loved and accepted by him on a more consistent basis.

I believed my father loved me the best he knew how. When we would see each other, he made me feel like I mattered to him—*my little girl* as he would call me. He lived out of state, creating greater distance and more excuses as to why we couldn't spend as much time together. When we'd speak on the phone my heart would nearly burst out of my chest as the conversations would come to a close because I could never be sure when I would hear his voice again. I remember spending half the summer with him when I was 14 years old and feeling as though I was on top of the world, never wanting it to end. Each time we would see each other, I would bask in those precious moments.

In the year 2000 my father decided to move from Virginia back to Maryland. Imagine my excitement knowing my daddy was coming to stay! He moved in with me for about two years, but during those years he was back and forth between houses. When my natural father whom

I could see and touch was not a constant in my daily life it made it even more difficult to trust the father I could not see. How could I believe I was so adored and loved by God the Father when my earthly father showed me something completely different?

After reading Psalm 139 and reflecting on the words God spoke to my former supervisor, "Tell Monica I love her," I was able to realize how much God knew and loved me despite my setbacks, the epiphany hit me and changed the correlation of my natural and spiritual relationship with the two. I no longer associated the relationship with my natural father as the same with my spiritual one.

Realizing God knew me because He created my entire life's purpose before I physically existed was life-changing for me. He knew what, when, and how I was going to do things in my life. When I went left instead of heading right, He had an alternative plan for that. I could not explain a life that only He had the answers to. My life was inevitably purposed and designed for His glory; it did not look the way I planned or desired.

I spent countless years trying to figure Me out and explain to others what I could not understand. God knew my ways, He knew me even as I slept and when I was awake. He's known all of my thoughts before they were manifested. He knew how to interpret the thoughts I would have of Him, others, and myself before they actually occurred. Yet I assumed my choice of lifestyle somehow was all He was concerned with when it came to me.

With all the twists and turns in my life, God still

had a strategic plan for me that I was unaware of. He knew my heart's desires better than anyone and yet I was afraid to speak to Him. I did not know how to converse with Him about a life I chose instead of the one I thought He designed for me. Being transparent with Him seemed impossible. *It is amazing what the mind will allow you to believe when you are the most vulnerable.*

How dare I believe He ever stopped loving me as if I were not an image of Him? I was reminded that I was fearfully and wonderfully made. I was perfect in His sight and I was His masterpiece, uniquely designed and set apart for His purpose. My very steps were ordered by Him, designed as He intended. The thought of this freed my soul, making me able to understand His love again.

I can't recall the countless times He led me through my fear and doubt, misery and weakness. When I realized He was in the same place I left Him when I walked away, I was stunned. I caused my suffering, my agony, my pain by thinking I was alone all this time. Redefining my personal relationship with God in my own way was refreshing, to say the least. The closer I became to Him again, the more love I felt. The dead weight lifted off my shoulders. The loneliness and the deep depression gave me a greater appreciation of being back together with Him again. The hole that was in my heart had been replaced with his undying and everlasting love.

God's love is the same yesterday, today, and forever (Hebrews 13:8 KJV). I thought I needed to be this perfect person in order for God to keep loving me. I never understood, until I had to, that I spent so much time trying to change my exterior that I neglected my interior, which is my heart where God dwells. I may not have it all together, but His Love did not give up on me and it won't give up on you. He loves everything about me and you in a way that seems impossible. Remember we were made in His likeness; when He looks at us He sees Himself.

Never allow yourself to believe God could stop loving you even if you never change.

CHAPTER 9
No More Questions
(Why Was I in Doubt?)

God has a way of teaching us lessons through unlikely sources and revealing His presence when we least expect it. I love telling this story as it was one of the first time I truly experienced trusting God. I remember being about 11 years old, watching my uncle play the lottery. It was like clockwork. I would look at his expression each time he missed a number or two and feel so bad—even as a child I understood that defeat never felt good.

One afternoon, I heard him come in and turn the television on; he always waited for Channel 5 to announce the winning digits. I ran upstairs to my bedroom, dropped down on my knees and prayed to God, pleading with him to grant my uncle a winner that night. And as sure as I prayed, he won. I couldn't believe it, I was so excited! My prayers worked because He was listening, at least that is what I believed at the time. I told my uncle, "You won because I prayed for you." He thanked me and gave me five dollars; he believed my prayer worked too.

At a young age I came to the conclusion God was God. I've known and been close to God my entire life even when I didn't quite know why or understand. I had not been introduced to the God everyone else knew. He was just a God that could do anything, and that is how I saw Him. No protocol or order to my prayer, I just prayed with a pure and innocent heart.

I never felt the need to question God; He was God and I trusted Him. Later as I became a teenager, God was still someone I trusted and believed in. I still believed He was a person you consulted or prayed to when you needed something, whatever it was.

The older I got, the more uncertain I became of who I was and what my purpose was in this world. I was constantly second-guessing all of my decisions and people around me, fearing that I could trust no one. I was all too familiar with disappointment and my guard was high. Of course I started to question God whenever I would doubt myself; an inquisitive mind is an intelligent one, isn't it?

People's idea of God was projected onto me and it began to taint how I saw Him. No matter what I went through in my life prayer was always pivotal for me, and when I felt I could no longer pray because I decided to choose an alternative lifestyle questions about God and me became more apparent.

The condemning messages had outweighed any goodness in my heart about God. I had everything I wanted and asked for: love. It was just that the package it arrived in threw me off. There she was, this beautiful person filling me with love like no other, and I was too afraid to fully receive it because of the way I was made to feel for loving Her.

All the noise ringing in my ears had told me how disgusting I was for choosing Her and how I was a disgrace before God. The noise represented the language and thoughts the enemy had planted in my head; it kept me from believing I was deserving of God's love. My voice had become silenced because of my fears, and that's how the outside noise was able to overpower my truth about God's amazing grace. I had to get to a place of peace about my decision and stop questioning the love God had for me.

Accepting What It Was

I was in love and my dreams had come true; I was not willing to walk away from Her. She fulfilled me, making me feel alive and loved again. We both laughed at the same things until our bellies hurt and enjoyed the same foods. We completed each other's sentences and read one another's mind as we thought out loud. Our love was genuine and heartfelt. We complimented each other and encouraged growth.

I had previously spoken to God during the time being separated from my ex-husband about someone loving me as He did. I never imagined this love would come in the form of a woman. I often wondered how a woman could love me so much without any reservation. I was in a constant battle questioning His love for me, and the conflict needed to stop. I had been all over the place trying to live for others while trying to create my own happiness. Trying to please them all, I displeased myself instead. Reconfiguring my brain, adjusting its focus was a task, but one that I had no choice in getting done.

I was refined gold, pure and luminous; I was loved and adored by God. When I lived my life for other flawed individuals, I lived a polished lie and no longer found peace in the world. I came to grips that my life was not created for people, but for God. I decided I would live for the creator, flaws and all, because he already knew my beginning and end. I did not have to answer to other people about who I was or had not yet become.

I desired to love God, therefore, I started trusting the process, believing in God's strategy for how my life should be built. I could no longer live expecting others to understand what God allowed or purposed for me when they were struggling to walk their own path. I could no longer wallow in my insecurities; I had to live and love without boundary the way God had planned.

Questions were no longer necessary. I knew who He was, and in return He knew me. This was satisfying enough for me to live, laugh, and love while basking in the greater years to come, all within the presence of my savior's endless love and grace. Although our struggles might be similar, my story is not intended to give you permission to live life as I am living mine. You might be struggling with where you are as I still do at times, but continue in the race and don't quit.

In the end, I hope that you will be able to stand in your truth and be honest about wherever you find yourself in life. Life for you may be complicated as it was for me. Your family might not look like mine, or maybe it does. But no matter where you find yourself, I say live without an explanation, live with a purpose, and live knowing God loves you no matter what.

No matter how you feel trust God in it, through it, and out of it. Don't allow your circumstances to smother or suffocate you. Push through what you don't understand, allow God to pull you through when you feel stuck, and trust even when you can't believe.

Proverbs 3:5-6
(New International Version)

Trust in the Lord with all your heart and lean not on your own understanding; in all your ways submit to him, and he will make your paths straight.

As I already said, "God is not done with me yet and this is not the end of my story."

ABOUT THE BOOK

Almost 15 years ago my life changed forever. I entered into a relationship that went against all I had been taught. The struggles, convictions (and most of the time) condemnations left me crippled in every way: mentally, emotionally, and spiritually.

After much prayer and reaffirming myself, I was able to accept God's divine love again just as I did when I was a child. I was reintroduced to Him during the most crucial time in my life and got to know who He really is. I gained strength, resilience, and the true experience of God's love for me in spite of my shortcomings. Not only was I able to receive love, but I learned how to give it.

I'm unapologetically ME despite all that I have been through. This gave me permission to recognize the gifts, talents, qualities, and greatness that lay dormant during that season of doubt. I hope my story gives you the courage and strength to be FREE in who you are because being bound just won't do. Wherever you are in your life, may the peace of God be there with you. Above all things never forget that He loves you and has a great plan for your life through your story.

Jeremiah 29:11, *"For I know the plans I have for you, declares the Lord, plans to prosper you and not harm you, plans to give you hope and a future."*

ABOUT THE AUTHOR

Monica Williams is a native of Baltimore, Maryland, who now resides in the state of Pennsylvania. She is the founder and visionary behind Women Empowering Women to Be Women of Truth, an organization that motivates women to become their authentic self by unveiling and removing the masks we parade around in publicly. She is also a member of Nikkie Pryce's I AM Community.

Monica earned a Bachelor of Arts and a Master of Arts in Social Work, both from Millersville/Shippensburg University. She also studied at the Maryland Theological Seminary in Baltimore.

Monica and her spouse have five children and two grandchildren and enjoy vacationing, cooking, watching movies, fellowshipping, and spending time with family and friends. She is always thinking of ways she can improve in her personal, professional, and spiritual life as she becomes the best version of herself in her quest to be the image of God in every way possible. One of her favorite scriptures is Luke 1:45, *"Blessed is she who has believed that the Lord would fulfill His promises to her."*

Contact Monica:
Instagram: wew_womenoftruth
Email: womenoftruth14@gmail.com
Website: www.womenoftruthco.com

BOOK MONICA TO SPEAK!

Monica Williams is the founder and visionary behind Women Of Truth, an organization that encourages and elevates other women to be an example and representation of their authentic self. In the words of Shakespeare, "To thine own self-be true."

Monica meets and speaks with women discussing topics such as:

Are You A Polished Mess?
Loving The Real You
What Women Want, What Men Need
Fathered vs Fatherless Daughters
What's Taboo to You?
The Walking Wounded
The Necessary Mask
Come as You Are and Tell it Like it is

Become a member today and attend our women empowerment events by visiting womenoftruthco.com

Connect with Monica!

www.womenoftruthco.com

wew_womenoftruth

womenoftruth14@gmail.com

CPSIA information can be obtained
at www.ICGtesting.com
Printed in the USA
BVHW040303090119
537384BV00006B/14/P